GW00870448

Tel Aviv
Walks

Claudia Stein

Disclaimer:
I do not assume any liability for the accuracy and currentness of the
information provided throughout this book, nor for the contents on the
cited websites. No law was being violated at the moment of publishing.

ISBN-13: 978-1516837014
ISBN-10: 1516837010

Edition: 02

TABLE OF CONTENTS

IN MEMORIAM

Max Eduard Richter

23 July 1877 – 10 October 1936

Murdered by the Nazis.
Burried as suicide.

Preface

Tel Aviv is not only an amazing city; its history reads like a thriller. The sand dunes and the swamps are gone, but history is all around wherever you go; the Ottomans, the International Style architecture, the Templers…you cannot escape.

The extraordinary past and vibrating present can be easily explored through city walks, sightseeing by bus and guided walks, which are offered for free by the municipality. On all walks you will come by many restaurants and cafés, so you can interrupt your walk at any time and take life easy.

Tel Aviv, February 2017

Claudia Stein

http://www.stein-books.com

check for updates!

1   In A Nutshell

1.1   Israel

Official Name: Medinat Yisrael = State of Israel

Telephone Country Code: +972, mobile phones +972-5

Internet: .co.il

Time Zone: UTC +2

Currency: New Israeli Shekel (NIS)

Founding of State: 5 Iyar 5708 (14 May 1948)

Form of Government: Parliamentary republic

National Independence Holiday: 5. Iyar

Capital and Seat of Government: Jerusalem

Official Languages: Modern Hebrew (Ivrit), Arabic

Population: ca. 8.18 Mio (May 2014)

Area: 22,072 km² / 8,522 mi² (without autonomous regions)

Religions: Judaism (75.3%), Islam (20.5 %), other (4.2%)

National Anthem: HaTikwa (Eng.: "The Hope")

Biggest City: Jerusalem (ca. 775,000 residents)

1.2   Short Bio of Tel Aviv

Official Name: Tel Aviv-Yafo

Telephone City Code: 03

Founded: 11 April 1909 as Achuzat Beit

*Area: 51.4 km²/ 19.9 mi², metro area: 1,516 km²/ 585 mi²

Population: ca. 400,000 (city), ca. 3.3 million (metro area)

Religions (municipal area): Judaism 91%, Islam 3%, Christianity 1%, other 5%

2   Urban History

The official name of the city is Tel Aviv-Yafo. This little hyphen connects more than just two words, it connects two different worlds with painful memories. The history of ancient Jaffa can well be traced until the 19th century. Much less was documented in the last 150-200 years and many of those documents only exist in Arabic, which means that most people in the western world have no access to this information. The research of the history of Tel Aviv was also a challenge to the historians but for very different reasons. The history of the city, which many claim it does not even have, is shrouded in mystery. Legend has it that it was a suburb of Jaffa that miraculously became a metropolitan city over the years. Others say that Tel Aviv had been built by German Jews who fled Nazi Germany, hence all the Bauhaus buildings. There are many other versions around but so far, none has told the historical facts or considered the political environment of that time which shows the founding of the city in a totally new and even more impressive perspective.

Only in the last 10-15 years have historians, architects and city planners – Israelis and foreigners –started searching for the traces of the city and its origins. The wish to get the architecture recognized by UNESCO (achieved in 2003) reinforced the need for documentation. At the beginning of the 20th century there were many languages spoken in the area — English, Hebrew, German, Yiddish, Russian and Arabic — and therefore, all documents that were finally found were in different languages. Arabic was mainly used to purchase land from wealthy Arabic owners who mostly did not even live in Palestine and to whom those sand dunes were of little value. The political changes had added another burden to the project. Old maps were the hardest to find and if found, to categorize. Maps and documents from the period of the British Mandate (1918-1948) have practically completely disappeared or had been moved from Tel Aviv to Jerusalem and nobody has ever found them again. At the same time, it was customary to change street names and personal names to Hebrew. Still today, new immigrants are allowed to change their names once they come to Israel. There are still doubts in many cases if two names on different documents refer to the same person or not.

2.1 Jaffa

According to one of the many legends, Jaffa was founded by Yophet (Arabic: Yafet), one of the three sons of Noah and one of the eight survivors of the Noachian flood. The exact year is not documented. Excavations have shown that there are eight different settlements below the Jaffa we know it today, witnesses of roughly 3,800 years of history. It is yet unclear who those settlers were but they were not the same during the whole time; for the last 4,000 years people were moving in and out. The harbor of Jaffa had turned the city into a regional economic center from its earliest years. It had brought the city wealth and international trade relations.

Already early in its history, the natural harbor turned Jaffa into an important economic center in the region. The city became rich, cosmopolitan and also the desire of all rulers at that time. The Canaanites, the Philistines, King David and his son King Salomon, Napoleon and the Ottomans – they all had an eye on Jaffa. At the end of the 13th century ACE, after successfully defeating the Crusaders at the harbor, the Mamelukes destroyed the harbor to prevent their enemies from coming back. The Ottomans captured Palestine at the beginning of the 16th century and controlled it until Napoleon arrived in 1799. The area increased in prosperity and the harbor was renewed.

During this period numerous Christian pilgrims arrived by boat in Jaffa on their way to Jerusalem. When Egyptian Muhammad Ali Pasha conquered Jaffa, wealthy Egyptian families decided to immigrate. In the following years, Jews from Northern Africa and Turkey also found their way to Jaffa. Slowly but steadily, Jewish life came back again. Those Jews who had already been in the country for quite some time belonged to the Sephardim. Their ancestors had fled from Spain and Portugal and their lifestyle was very oriental. The Ashkenazim – from Middle and Eastern Europe – had not been in the country before ca. 1840. Most could not maintain themselves, lived mainly for the study of the Torah and were dependant on payments from the diaspora. When the Ottomans defeated Muhammad Ali Pasha in 1841, Jaffa became an economic center once more. The construction of the Jaffa light house in 1865 was very foresightful: only 4 years later in 1869, the Suez Canal opened and Jaffa became even more important, soon even indispensible: the growing production of Jaffa oranges were exported to many countries.

In the meantime (September 1866) George Jones Adams, founder of the "Church of the Messiah," and his 156 followers had come from Boston to Jaffa. They bought a plot of land, erected the wooden prefabricated houses they had brought from home and started a community in the north of Jaffa that can still be seen today around Bar Hoffman Street. None of them had been prepared for the hardship of agricultural life abroad and only a few months later, in winter 1867 most of them wanted to leave Jaffa and go back home. The majority of them had already left when in the beginning of 1869 some Southern German "Templers" arrived and offered to buy from Adams' group their settlement that would later be known as the "(American-) German Colony of Jaffa." The Templers founded a new settlement east of Jaffa in 1871, Sarona. At the same time there were plans to open a railway connection from Jaffa to Jerusalem and in 1888, the Templers added another little compound close to the future train station. The railway line was opened in 1892. The construction of the railway confirmed Jaffa's status and brought even more business activities to the city.

The old train station, "HaTachana," was renovated a couple of years ago and is a nice and lively place with coffee shops, restaurants and boutiques today. The train station was located in the former urban Arabic quarter of Manshiye that was demolished in the 1960s. In 1870s the first sections of the old city wall were torn down to prepare for future expansion. A new urban district developed in the north of Jaffa, right next to the beach: Manshiye. The Charles Clore Park stands on the former western part of this quarter. The Jewish citizens of Jaffa moved further north and founded Neve Tzedek, Hebrew for "Oasis of Justice," (1887) and Neve Shalom, Hebrew for "Oasis of Peace" (1890.) The stand-alone Etzel Museum is one of the last witnesses to history as well as the train station itself, the Red House next to it and last but not least the Hassan Bek Mosque. After the demolition the municipality had planned to erect the Tel Aviv Business District here. But these plans were later abandoned and today the business district can be found at the border of Ramat Gan, next to the Ayalon Highway. Other new quarters from this time are Ajami and Jabaliya in the south and Souza and Salameh in the east. It was a time of a blossoming economy and more foreigners from many different countries would immigrate. The Maronite and Coptic Christians started to populate Ajami where you can still today find many churches built in those days.

In summer 1914 Hassan Bek became the new mayor of Jaffa and the mosque of Manshiye – built in 1916 – bears his name. Bek had a vision; he wanted to modernize the country and the big and wide Boulevards the Europeans had introduced to the Middle East served him as a model. After the break-out of World War I he expelled all Russian citizens from Jaffa. Russia was the arch-enemy of Turkey and Bek feared conflicts in Jaffa. Those very Russian citizens were almost exclusively Jewish, hence the expulsion caused a chorus of outrage among the Jewish communities, including those in Europe. Soon Bek was renowned for his rigorous and brutal clampdown. Legend has it that he would arrest people in the street and force them to work for his city development projects. This course of action also led to the relocation of some Muslim cemeteries which is against the religious law. Tel Aviv's Rothschild Boulevard became the model for Jaffa's Jerusalem Boulevard, at that time named "Jamal Pasha Boulevard." Pasha was the governor of Syria since 1915. After two years in office, Bek was removed.

The "Pioneers' House," a Jewish hostel in Yefet Street, also became one of the targets during the excesses of 1921. An Arabic mob had forced their entry into the house and even local police did not stop them. A Jewish policeman who came by accidentally put the aggressors to flight by the use of his gun. At this point, 14 guests were already dead and the others were hiding on the second floor. A few weeks later the hostel moved to Allenby Street. The consistent assaults provoked the British rulers to broaden the streets in Jaffa to make them easier to patrol with military vehicles; about 250 houses were demolished.

In the two-state-solution, a suggestion from the UN published in November 1947, Jaffa was supposed to be an enclave on Jewish territory. But at this time the two parties were already at war with each other and the UN solution did not seem feasible any longer. The Brits decide to leave Palestine. In November 1947 the first mass exodus set in. About 30,000 Arabs left Jaffa, mainly for Gaza and Beirut. The conflict between Jews and Arabs became even more heated. In January 1948 the Jewish resistance bombed the Saray building, the seat of the Arab administration and End of April the "Irgun" (also called "Etzel") took over Manshiye. In the days following this event the fighters of the Hagana movement conquered the villages outside Jaffa. The British military showed a massive presence in Jaffa but the last 70,000 citizens decided to leave. On 13 May 1948 Jaffa surrendered and the remaining 3,000 people of the former metropolitan city gathered in Ajami. After the founding of the State of Israel on 14 May 1948 the Jews were expelled from the neighboring Arab countries; another mass exodus set in, this time to Jaffa, where only weeks before the Arab population had casted off. They arrived in a deserted town and settled wherever they found a place.

In the 1950s the new developments started in Jaffa and not very much was preserved. Since 1950 Tel Aviv and Jaffa are united and the city's official name is Tel Aviv-Yafo. The many immigrants changed the face of the city and new houses mushroomed everywhere. In the original plans high-rise buildings were supposed to give room to the new citizens; nobody seemed to be interested in preserving anything from the past. Manshiye was completely erased from the landscape in 1963 when the last ruins were demolished. When the harbor of Ashkelon opened in 1965, the golden times of the Jaffa port were finally over and the area became desolate. It was a group of artists who would convince then-mayor Shlomo Lahat in the 1970s to preserve Jaffa. Until today Jaffa is affected by social conflicts, especially because of rising prices for housing.

The recent renovations and new construction attract a wealthier and Jewish audience and the local population feels threatened. This forms an excellent breeding ground for Islamic groups. Since 1999 the municipality is investing in the revitalization of Jaffa, a term that does not mean the same to all involved. Today, not much remains of the former Jaffa. The authentic Jaffa can still be found, but only in the hidden little streets, off the beaten tourist path.

Jaffa remains a sore point in the Mideast conflict. Jaffa was the pride of the Arabic population. Why was it abandoned? The reasons are manifold; one is that the Jews had been fed up since the consistent assaults in 1921 and the Arab population feared revenge. The British police had their own daily fight with the Jewish resistance groups and nobody had any confidence in them protecting Jaffa and its population. The Jewish elite had prepared their independence for decades while the Arabs were without a leader and organizational structure. It had been a catastrophe – nakba – to abandon Jaffa. The "Bride of the Sea" as they called the city, had been the political and cultural cradle of the population. Intellectuals and rich merchants had lived here, where the most important newspapers of Palestine were once published. Feelings of anger, impotence and humiliation come up again when they think of Jaffa.

2.2 Tel Aviv

The oldest and still visible part of Tel Aviv is not Neve Tzedek, it is the Templer settlement "Sarona", locally known as HaKirya ("the campus.") After the founding of the State of Israel in May 1948 this area served as the first government seat of the young state. Another settlement – Mount Hope, founded in 1849 – is unfortunately not visible anymore. It was located close to today's motorway junction LaGuardia Interchange in the south of Tel Aviv on the campus of the Shva Mofet High School (HaMasger

Street.) The city development has also been significantly influenced by every Aliya, the Jewish immigration to Israel. On 11 April 1909 the newly acquired plots of land, sand dunes, were split among the new owners and the construction of the first houses began. The motivation for this very project can be best understood in the historical context.

Mount Hope (1849–1853)
In the middle of the 19th century many Christians in the US and Europe were convinced that the Messiah would come back soon. A group of German and American Christians, among them the John Steinbeck's German grandparents, came into the country and together they founded the settlement of Mount Hope in 1849. Their mission consisted of teaching the local Jews agriculture and Christianity. Moses Montefiori, a British-Jewish philanthropist, visited the Holy Land to buy plots of land and finally purchased the Mount Hope orchid plantations from Rabbi Yehuda HaLevi. The area is still called the Montefiori quarter. On the night of 11 January 1858, the Christian settlers were attacked by a group of Arabs without any previous incident or warning. The village was looted, some men were murdered and their wives raped. The reasons for this brutal assault have never been identified. Interviewed by the Police, the settlers would say that they believe that their successful farming had been the subject of envy among the Arab neighbors. Nevertheless, only a few months later, they would abandon their mission in the Holy Land and move together to the USA.

The German Templers (1869-1949)
When Tel Aviv started looking into its own young history, the Templers would surface again. They were the group that had most significantly influenced the development of the country and served as a model for the founders of Tel

Aviv. They had the most modern houses, applied the latest technology in all their activities and managed to live absolutely independently in the Holy Land. They did not see their mission in teaching Christianity to Jews or Muslims, rather being a living example by living an exemplary life, preferably in the Holy Land, the home of Jesus Christ. This is how they had defined their goal when they split from the National Church in 1861. Christoph Hofmann (1815-1885) and his followers founded their own church – The Temple Society – in Kirschenhardthof, a village 40 km north-east of Stuttgart in Southern Germany (Baden-Württemberg.) The Templers are often mistaken for the Knights Templar, a Christian military order that was active in the 12th century and responsible for the Crusades, but they have nothing more in common than the name.

In 1867 a small group from Germany did not want to wait any longer and decided to move to the Holy Land, without any support from the other Templers. They settled in the Jezreel Valley in the north of the country, between the Galilee and Samaria – a fatal decision. In this sparsely populated area most of them would die in the following years, mainly from malaria. After this tragedy the Temple Society planned very carefully and strategically to where to move. The following settlements were finally realized:

Haifa: 1869
Jaffa: 1869 (purchase of the American settlement)
Sarona: 1871 (purchase of 60 hectares of non-arable land from Arabic owner)
Neuhardthof: 1888 (extension of Haifa)
Walhalla: 1888 (extension of Jaffa)
Rephaim: 1873 (close to Jerusalem)
Wilhelma: 1902 (today Bnei Atarot)
Bethlehem: 1906

After the purchase of the American settlement in 1869, the Templers bought the plots that were later known as Sarona, east of Jaffa. Today Kaplan Street crosses the former Sarona and connects Dizengoff Square with the Azrieli Center and its surrounding business district. At the end of the 19th century people from all over would immigrate to Palestine; Muslims, Jews, Christians, but none of these groups invested so much of their energy and knowledge into the future of this geographical area. The Templers stood out. The hygienic situation of Palestine was a challenge for everybody, but especially for the new immigrants, illnesses like malaria made it even worse. The Sarona plots were especially difficult to cultivate and many were sick. The Templers decided to import eucalyptus trees to drain the swamps. The layout of Sarona was planned strategically: the purchased plots were divided into lots, the new owners determined by lottery. Everybody had enough space to build a home with a little garden. The construction was subject to previously determined rules. Interestingly enough, this was not the last "creative urban planning"; the founders of Tel Aviv would do exactly the same in April 1909: subdivide the plots, establish rules for construction and determine the owners by lottery. The founders of Tel Aviv had studied the Templers very closely, especially their buildings were considered all-time modern. Everywhere in the country where the Templers were active, the general living conditions improved in a short time for everybody living in that area. This was the main motivation for Arabs from other areas to move here. From the Templers they learned efficient agriculture or found work on their plantations. The Templers were completely independent. They cultivated their own oranges, fruits, wine, had cattle breeding and dairies. Among the Templers all kind of professions could be found and their specialists and skilled workers were very popular and busy outside the Templer Society.

During the economic boom Jaffa started expanding outside the original city walls and also the Templers kept an eye out for new plots. They found a well located area right on the border between Neve Tzedek and Jaffa near where the train was supposed to run in the near future. Here they built their industry (e.g. the water pump factory of Wilhelm and Georg Wagner) and some housing.

The Templers were proud Germans but they considered Palestine "home." None of them had ever thought of going back to Germany; they had invested so much energy and money here, giving up was simply not an option. Since they had dissociated themselves from the German National Church they did not get financial help from anybody, unlike other Christian missions. The reclaiming of the plots and the life they had built was their very own success and they felt like they were a part of the country. Until the end of 1917 Palestine was ruled by the Ottomans. The Turks were quite suspicious of foreigners and other religions but the Templers refused the Ottomans' offer to exchange their German passports for Turkish ones even though this could have gained them many advantages in daily life, especially when permits were needed. On the other hand the Ottomans recognized the Templers' expertise in many areas like the British later did. Several bridges and train stations in Palestine were built by the Templers' engineer Josef Wennagel.

At the end of World War I the British had defeated the Ottomans and life would dramatically change for the Templers, gradually leading to the end of their existence in Palestine. The British accused them of spying for Germany and Turkey and decided to deport them. Most of them would spend the following two years in Helouan, close to Cairo, Egypt. Back in Palestine they would find their settlements in deplorable state. Their houses were looted, the factories and plantations neglected. Nevertheless, the Templers rolled up their sleeves and built it up once again.

In the 1920s more and more Jews immigrated to Palestine, some following the Zionist dream, others fleeing the uprising anti-Semitism especially in Eastern Europe. This development would lead to even more resentments among the Arab population who felt seriously threatened by the Jewish salesmanship which resulted in an increasing number of assaults against Jews. The Templers remained neutral. They needed the Arab labor and the Jewish clients, but their German nationalism helped the Nazi party (NSDAP) undermine the community. The keeping of German traditions was the perfect stepping stone for the introduction of Nazi ideology which caused tensions among the Templers. Not every Templer was by definition pro-Nazi only because he worshipped in German and wanted to keep national traditions alive. Many saw a contradiction between Nazi ideology and Christian teaching. But most of them did believe that a strong Germany would be helpful for Germans living abroad. In this context it is no surprise that there would later be groups of the Hitler Youth (Hitlerjugend) in Jaffa, a shock for those Jews who had barely escaped Nazi Germany and hardly made it to Palestine because of the British immigration quota that was intended to appease the Arab population and keep all options open in the Middle East where oil had been found. Sarona was located outside Jaffa and most of the time the Templers would take a moped or a bike to Jaffa. How could they show the Arab snipers that they were not Jews? The Nazi flag with the swastika was well understood.

With the beginning of World War II and the involvement of the United Kingdom it was time to act on the British Mandate of Palestine. The Templers were only good for one reason: they supplied the British with good food including excellent wine, but they were Germans and Germany was the enemy. It was simply unacceptable having the enemy in their own territory. At the same time the overall situation in Palestine became ungovernable: the Jews were hostile against the German Templers because of their affinity with the Nazis, the Arabs attacked the Jews – and often also the British as an expression of their disappointment that their collaboration against the Ottomans had not brought them the promised independence. The British decided to start with the Templers though they had no idea to where to deport them; most of them were born in Palestine.

The Wagner family belonged to those Templers who had already been pro-Arab in 1921 during the Arab assaults. Later they would openly sympathize with the Nazis. Even though they had also been interned in an enemy aliens' camp, the British allowed them to re-open their factories after 1945. The Jews were outraged; after the war the atrocities of the Nazis were known all over the world. In March 1946, Gotthilf Wagner was murdered on Levanda Street. The authorities suspected a Jewish resistance group behind this unsolved murder case.

In the following years the deportees were shipped from one camp to another and back to Sarona, only few deciding to move to Germany. In 1948 they are finally transported to Famagusta, Cyprus, and later, in 1948, to Australia.

First Aliya (1882–1903)
The first Aliya of the Zionist would ultimately overwhelm Jaffa. Haifa and Jaffa were the only harbors at the shallow coastline and therefore, the first arrival place of all immigrants from which many of them would not want to move on. The ancient city with its narrow little streets was

23

soon about to collapse. The housing shortage was severe and hygiene practically absent; the lack of a sewage system would make things even worse. Living in Jaffa would soon turn into a realistic threat to one's health. The European Jews in particular could not see themselves adapt to this kind of life. A group of wealthy Sephardic Jews decided to build a new settlement outside Jaffa and bought plots of land. In 1887, the first Jewish settlement outside Jaffa was founded: Neve Tzedek (Hebrew for "Oasis of Justice") and in 1890, Neve Shalom (Hebrew for "Oasis of Peace") would follow. The latter was built right next to Neve Tzedek for the less wealthy.

Herzl and the dream of "The Jewish State" (1896–1904)
Theodor Herzl (1860–1904), in Israel Binyamin Herzl was an Austro-Hungarian writer and journalist and is considered the founder of international Zionism. When his book "The Jewish State" (in German "Der Judenstaat") was published in February 1896, in Vienna, nobody could have even dreamed that this was the blueprint of the Jewish State to come and not only an essay on Zionism. Herzl's description of the Jews' misery, the necessity for their own state and his vision on the future political development is so much beyond belief as is the timeliness that is impressed on today's reader. Herzl draws a blueprint on how to establish a Jewish state and most of it was realized in the exact same way, here in Tel Aviv. It was the first Jewish city, founded by Jews and constructed by Jews for Jews. It was the first capital of Israel and a test field for everything to come. Nearly all institutions that were founded with the aim of the establishment of a Jewish state were located in Tel Aviv. Here the corner stones were laid for a new Jewish society; a free society, independent from non-Jews and self-determined, not reduced to its religion but recognizing the religious values as its pillars. Many of the European Jews were not very religious but the society they lived in

and for which they had fought in wars did not integrate them; they were simply Jews. Herzl described it in the following way:

Attacks in Parliaments, in assemblies, in the press, in the pulpit, in the street, on journeys--for example, their exclusion from certain hotels--even in places of recreation, become more numerous daily. The forms of persecution vary according to the countries and social circles in which they occur. In Russia, imposts are levied on Jewish villages; in Romania, a few persons are put to death; in Germany, they get a good beating occasionally; in Austria, Anti-Semites exercise terrorism over all public life; in Algeria, there are traveling agitators; in Paris, the Jews are shut out of the so-called best social circles and excluded from clubs. Shades of anti-Jewish feeling are innumerable. The book provoked very different reactions among Jews and non-Jews but what annoyed Herzl most was that it would be classified as utopia. His book picks up the "Jewish Question" that – according to Herzl – has not been given a solution since the Middle Ages. At the end of every Pessah celebration Jews say "Next year in Jerusalem!"

Since the destruction of the Second Temple in the year 70 CE and the Romans coming into power, the Jews have been dreaming of coming back to their country and to found the State of Israel in the Land of Israel. Even in times of uncertainty and prosecution the Jews always hesitated to leave the country they were living in; they simply did not know where to go and this would not change if they did not have their own State. Herzl drew a concrete and detailed roadmap that was based on two pillars: the Society of Jews and the Jewish Company. He also suggested several ways to finance this project.

The task of the Society of Jews was primarily to build the nation and to prepare the political and economic conditions while the Jewish Company should take care of their execution. Palestine was chosen as this future home due to the historic Jewish ties to this piece of land. According to Herzl the land was the only resource that required approval from outside the community. He was confident that those countries with strong anti-Semitism would happily support a Jewish state. He knew that the country was mostly not arable. He suggests that the poorest of the poor immigrate first. They had never lost their belief in the Holy Land and nothing tied them to their country of residence except misery. Russia and Romania seemed to be ideal for the first recruitment.

The main tasks of the Jewish Company were the acquisition of land under private law that later should be guaranteed under international law. The workers would construct their shared residences for each other; simple and functional accommodation. The apartment block in Frishman Street 33-35 is an example of those days. Those workers were supposed to build up the whole country, starting with the residence and continuing with the infrastructure. An incoming agency would filter the stream of immigrants and they would settle next to their work. The remaining Jewish assets that could not be taken to Palestine would be listed for potential sale to Christians.

At the end of August 1897, Herzl held the World Congress of Zionism in Basle where the Basle Program was agreed: "Zionism seeks the creation of a secure home for the

Jewish people under public law." On 3 September 1897, Herzl wrote into his diary: "If I summarize the congress of Basle in one word – which I will be wary of saying out loud in public – it will be this: in Basle I founded the Jewish State. If I said that in public I would face a broad laughter. Maybe in 5 years, but definitely in 50 years, they will all agree."

Second Aliya (1904–1914)

This is one of the most important periods in regard to the founding of Tel Aviv. It is the time when the founding fathers immigrate. Still today the historians are wondering if "Achuzat Beit" as Tel Aviv was called at the beginning, was meant to be only a suburb with little nice gardens or whether this was only the embryo of the already imagined Jewish metropolis à la Herzl, a Jewish city for a Jewish state. We will never know. But it is a fact that Tel Aviv was not founded to leave Jaffa, this is what Neve Tzedek and Neve Shalom were for. The immigrating Europeans from places like Odessa, Kiev, Berlin and Budapest could simply not adapt to the Oriental way of life. In 1904, the Kerem HaTeimanim (vineyard of the Yemenites) neighborhood was founded by immigrants from Yemen. They were Zionists, too, but not in a political way and their lifestyle was more in tune with the oriental culture. Under the auspices of Akiva Aryé Weiss the building society "Achuzat Beit" was founded in 1906 with the main purpose of building this new suburb of which the Europeans had been dreaming. The current Jewish suburbs were too oriental to fuel immigration from Europe: still no sewage system, the streets were dirty and most public spaces neglected. The settlement of the Templer Society, Sarona, was a model the founders studied meticulously. Sarona was the embodiment of modernity and it had a European look and feel. It was no wonder that on 11 April 1909, the distribution of the lots of land to the first 66 families had been organized the Templers' way. The rules for the new owners were similar. They were allowed to build as they liked on their own piece of land with only few restriction, e.g. only one third of the space could be built on. For the public spaces, it was necessary to appoint an architect. Like the Templers, the Ashkenazim had little relation with the sea and started to flatten the sand dunes with their back to the water. The first building was finished in October 1909, and in 1910 the suburb was renamed "Tel Aviv", the title Nachum Sokolow had given the Hebrew translation of Herzl's book "Altneuland."

The most prominent founding fathers were Meir Dizengoff (1861-1936, originally from Moldavia) and Akiva Aryé Weiss (1868-1947 from Belarus.) Dizengoff came to Jaffa in 1905. The charismatic and handsome business man soon gained influence in Jewish society. He invested in many different fields and would soon start buying plots of land outside Jaffa. Weiss arrived in Jaffa in 1906 coming from ?ód?, Poland. He was determined to execute Herzl's plan; a Jewish society needed a Jewish city. In his opinion the agricultural settlements and the embellishment of existing buildings was simply not enough. He envisioned a large Tel Aviv for a new society. The day of his arrival he went to the first local meeting. The popular demand of his ideas resulted in his assignment for the execution. The building society "Achuzat Beit" was founded and soon construction of the first buildings started. When "Achuzat Beit" was finished in 1910, Weiss could not find any supporters for his plans for expansion and he decided to leave and invest in his own projects. Weiss contributed significantly to the development of the country by founding several factories and companies, like the "Ora Hadasha" movie company. He was also the builder of the "Eden Cinema" and the first post office building of the city. Later he would initiate the "Diamond Club", the embryo of today's Diamond Exchange.

Dizengoff had been cooperating right from the beginning with the "Achuzat Beit" society for the purchase of land. In 1911 he became chief city planner and 1922, the city's first mayor. During the following years Dizengoff practically eliminated Weiss from history and promoted himself as the initiator of the city who had smartly led the development from suburb to metropolis. The fact that the first plans for expansions had come from Weiss was omitted as were the main contributions of the Scottish city planner Patrick Geddes.

The British government published the Balfour Declaration on 2 November 1917, shortly after General Allenby had conquered the city of Beer Sheva and ended the Ottoman reign. In the Balfour Declaration the British committed themselves to help the Jews get a national home. During the British Mandate, Jews were allowed to immigrate to Palestine but there was no support available in any other aspect.

Third Aliya (1919–1923)
The 1st of May of 1921 was the day Jews would not forget for a long time. It was the day of Arab assaults on Jewish demonstrators. Two Jewish groups violently clashed during Labor Day demonstrations. The demonstration of the Jewish Communist Party had been authorized, but the Workers' Union (today Israel's Workers' Party, then lead by David Ben-Gurion) had called for an unauthorized countermarch. Both groups were knocking each other

around when suddenly an Arab group gathered to beat up the Jews, the violence escalated and lead to shootings and more violence. The Arab Police ignored the incident. The Jews were in shock. The civil population organized themselves and sealed off Tel Aviv. In the days that followed they picked up the remaining Jews in Jaffa and cast out Arabs from Jewish neighborhoods. At the end Jaffa was purely Arabic, an apparent victory for the aggressors that would soon backfire. The "assaults of Jaffa" went on for three days, but in this first week of May, Jews were attacked by Arabs all over the country. Life would change forever.

After the assault, the British High Commissioner Lord Herbert Samuel soon reorganized the administration: in June 1921, Tel Aviv was granted some autonomy and could impose tax. Until 1923, it was still mandated by Jaffa, later it was gathered with Neve Tzedek, Neve Shalom and Kerem HaTeimanim as well as all the purchased plots. Jaffa, the economic center until then, got cut off and suddenly there was a real gap between clients and merchants. For the latter, it was much more difficult to swallow. The Jews would avoid Jaffa. The new municipality stressed on the expansion towards the Yarkon River in the north – without Arab labor – and opened new shops; the products were imported from Europe and the money, too. Jaffa sank into poverty. The port business "saved" Jaffa until 1933. This was the year when the Haifa port opened and the monopoly fell. The border between Jaffa and Tel Aviv was drawn on Daniel Street, south of the Yemenite Quarter, on the other side of Manshiye. This area was the scene of fights between Arabs and Jews since then, especially in the 1940s.

The development of Tel Aviv benefitted from the events that reminded many citizens of Herzl. Self-supply and the responsibility for the own safety were the immediate tasks to fulfill. All labor became exclusively Jewish and the clichés would disappear. Being able to plan the future had been a Jewish dream for too long and now, for the first time, they had the chance to take care of their own destiny. The new immigrants of the third Aliya had to live in tents on the plots in the north. The Palestine Land Development Company would from now on be in charge of the purchase of new land.

Fourth Aliya (1924-1929)

These were the golden days of Tel Aviv. The cultural life was booming and well educated Europeans immigrated. The municipality appointed the Scotsman Patrick Geddes as strategic city planner, a so far unknown profession. Patrick gave the development the necessary rebound. Until now, all the planning only considered those plots of land that had already been purchased. Geddes would freely draw a new map, disregarding land ownership. He concentrated on large north-south and east-west connections. Geddes was a biologist. He studied closely the relationship between beings, in this case: the citizens. Where did they go, on which ways, who met who? He identified big streets for the main traffic, the access to the houses where wives and mothers interacted were already significantly smaller. The ways to the bakery as well as to the parks were supposed to be short. Here, where mothers and children lived, main traffic should be avoided. Geddes was not Jewish but sympathized with Zionism. Although Tel Aviv was a secular city, they all wanted to live in a society based on Jewish values. They agreed that Jewish holidays would be days off and celebrated in public. A synagogue was not the center of daily life anymore but still a main part of the culture and, therefore, should be in reasonable reach. Geddes understood the task. He took all those elements together to lead Judaism from religion to culture. Theaters, libraries and boulevards were the new center of public life. He also examined the local climate and the challenges it presented. He was the first in planning cubic houses with roof terraces, not those architects who would later earn their diplomas in Europe. Geddes understood the Jews' search for a new, modern Jewish society and avoiding any impression of tightness. In his planning, he left out a considerable amount of space for green areas. The city was supposed to be light and the buildings should not remind of the European "Shtetls", away from walls and cemeteries. In 1925 he presented a plan in which he planned the city from Bograshov Street up to the Yarkon River, the eastern border was Ibn Gvirol Street.

From 1927, it became increasingly difficult to get a building permit from the authorities in Jerusalem because High Commissioner Lord Herbert Samuel had been replaced by Lord Plumer. More and more, the Brits would reduce Tel Aviv's newly gained autonomy, especially their finances. From now on, the city expansion had to rely on donations only instead of taxes. At the same time, land to buy was getting scarce and the municipality would pass a new bill that allowed the expropriation of land from owners to win space which was more needed than ever from 1933 onwards.

Fifth Aliya (1929-1939)
Tel Aviv was finally running out of space and at the same time new immigrants would flood the country. The British bureaucracy for building permits would slow down construction activities, the rest of the world was suffering from an economic crisis and not much money was sent to support the projects in Tel Aviv. It had turned into a vibrant, European-style city; most of the new European immigrants did not want to move on to other parts of the

country and stayed in Tel Aviv. As a result, it had become impossible to keep all the green areas that Geddes had planned. Even existing gardens and parks had to give way. According to reports from that time, between 1931 and 1935, the population had tripled and reached 120,000. In 1934, the Jewish National Fund was able to purchase new plots of land in the north. Hence, mainly immigrants from Germany and Hungary, where the majority of immigrants came from, would settle in this area. Though all the labor was Jewish, the unemployment rate was very high. The Jewish society would drift apart into European Jews (Ashkenazim) and Oriental Jews (Sephardim.) The Ashkenazim would live in the north, the Sephardim in the south. This has not changed through today, only the distribution of unemployment is different: today, there are more people in the south without a job. The new immigrants at that time would all go north. The German Jews had the most difficulties in adapting. Most of them had been very established with a "normal" life in Germany until the Nazis came to power, so adapting to their new home proved difficult, unlike the Eastern European Jews who had integrated well in the new land and picked up the language very fast. For the "Jeckes" (pronounced: yeckes), as the Germans were called – because they always kept their jacket on, even in the summer heat, and hardly spoke Hebrew – the Eastern Europeans had no respect.

1936 was an emotional year for Tel Aviv and Israel in general. It was the year when the Arabic Revolt started that would not stop until 1939. Their leader was the Grand Mufti of Jerusalem, Mohammed Amin al-Husseini, who was on friendly terms with Nazi Germany and had significantly introduced the idea of anti-Semitism in the Arab world. In Syria and Egypt, the Arab workers had already been successful with their work stoppage and negotiations on their independence from France, and the

33

British Crown had already been on their way. On 17 May 1936, the works for the new Tel Aviv port started. This was another step towards independence; there was no other harbor between Haifa and Jaffa. The coast is very shallow here and big ships came as close as they could, then the passengers as well as the goods had to be transshipped into small rowing boats. This business was nearly 100% Arabic. Since the assaults from 1921, confidence in the Arab neighbors had vanished and nobody could still imagine a peaceful co-existence. These worries were fueled by the massacres from Hebron and Safed in 1929, and the attacks would not stop in the years to come. The landing in the port of Jaffa would take longer with every ship that entered due to increasing immigration and the expansion of the local economy. Oftentimes, the ships would have to wait for several days for their unloading. On 13 December 1934, two ships collided with each other close to the Yarkon estuary in the north, hence, a lighthouse was built in January 1935, close to today's port. A new port was the only solution. The name of the street closest to the port refers to those days: "Shaar Zion Street", the gate of Zion. In 1949, the municipality started an expansion of the Tel Aviv harbor by deepening it. This way, ships could enter the port and did not have to be unloaded at sea. The Grand Mufti ended the Arab strike in October 1936, and one month later the British would found the Peel Commission to investigate the Arab Revolt.

1936 was also the year the municipality constructed the Ben-Gurion airport between Tel Aviv and Jerusalem that would initially be open only for military usage. The Peel Commission declared in July 1937 that the strong anti-Semitism among the Muslim population could lead to only one possible solution: the separation into two states. Even though the Jewish part was much smaller and the Arabs had already been granted the whole territory east of the Jordan river (today known as the "Kingdom of Jordan"), the Arabs refused and the Grand Mufti would start the revolt again. At the end of that year, there were mass revolts and assaults on Brits and Jews but this time the attackers came from the rural population. The mayor of Tel Aviv, Israel Roach, asked the British Mandate government for a permit to build an airport for Tel Aviv. Traveling had become a huge risk for Jews. The airport Sadeh Dov was inaugurated in 1938 and offered regular flights to Haifa. The results of the Peel Commission led the British to give major concessions to the Arabs. Most probably, this move was motivated by the Crown's interest in the Middle East and the assumption that the Jews would depend on them. The next steps would be cemented in the "White Paper of 1939": in the following 5 years, only a maximum of 75,000 Jews were allowed to immigrate; any higher number would be subject to Arab approval. At the same, time the purchase of land through Jews became very much restricted.

World War II (1939-1945)
On 9 September 1940, Tel Aviv suffered its first air bombing, and without any prior warning and medical infrastructure in place. It was a hit from Mussolini against the British. The damages were considerable and 137 people lost their lives. Most of the victims were "residents" of the tent settlements that were not even equipped to withstand a major storm. A memorial stone reminds of this incident on the corner of King George Street and Ben Zion Boulevard. Less than a year later, the Vichy regime sent bombs to Tel Aviv; this time 20 people died.

End of the Palestine Mandate (1947-1948)
The British government decided to give up their mandate in 1948. The years of 1948 and 1947 felt like civil war. Jewish resistance fighters and Arab snipers fought each other violently. In December 1947, the Jewish National

Fund managed to purchase the Templer compound of Sarona from the Mandate parliament. The municipality had now gained land of an important size. This was not for residential purposes; they were looking for the future government seat of the state they were about to create. The area was renamed HaKirya, the campus, and "Sarona" would not be heard or read for a long time. On 5 Iyar 5708 (14 May 1948), David Ben-Gurion formally proclaimed the establishment of the State of Israel. At the end of the same year, the decision was taken to group Jaffa and Tel Aviv in one city which finally happened in 1950. Until today, there is a still a north-south division in Tel Aviv, though the municipality is trying to modernize the southern districts, including Jaffa, but the local residents simply cannot keep up with the modernization. Rents are rising and many have to give way to residential luxury projects and live in poverty. The protests on Rothschild Boulevard in 2011 have shown that this problem is not limited to the southern districts only anymore.

2.2.1 Tel Aviv today

Tel Aviv can be roughly divided into 5 districts:
- North
- Northern Center
- Center
- South
- Jaffa

Patrick Geddes had planned the city up to the Yarkon Park, which for a long time was the city's northern border. Today, the **North** stops where Herzliya, the next city, begins. The stylish towers with its condominiums for the wealthier residents as well as the University are located north of the Park. Locals call the part between Ben-Gurion Boulevard and Yarkon Park the "old North", though correctly this would only apply to the area west of Ibn

Gvirol Street. Geddes' plan had not included the areas further east. The now closed-down Tel Aviv port is also located in the "**old North**" and offers night life, bars, restaurants, coffee shops right next to the sea. And last but not least, Dizengoff Street is a very prominent old-time witness with its elegant shops.

The famous Dizengoff Square with its classical International Style architecture is located in the **Northern Center**. Most of the buildings from the 1930s are located here. Between Ben-Gurion Boulevard and Bograshov Street, 75% of the buildings belong to the "White City" as defined by the UNESCO. Tel Aviv's **center** is rich in history. This is where everything began: the first houses of Achuzat Beit and the Rothschild Boulevard were located here, as well as the first Jewish high school. Later, in 1948, the State of Israel was formally proclaimed on Rothschild Boulevard No. 16. The center is also called "Lev HaIr" – heart of the city. The streets already existed in old plans from 1924, but some of the houses were constructed later.

The districts of Neve Tzedek and Florentin form the **South**. Shortly before the end of the century, Jaffa had started to expand. The Maronite Christians would found Ajami in the south of Jaffa, the Muslims went north and settled where today the Charles Clore Park can be found and the Jews founded Neve Tzedek. Some 30 years later, Florentin was founded by Greek Jews from Saloniki. The cornerstone for the Kerem HaTeimanim was laid in 1904 but because of its geographic location, it is not part of the South. Jaffa is also south, but it is mostly mentioned apart.

Jaffa, "the beauty", with its medieval history and the exceptional fusion of Arabic and European culture, different religions, architecture and ethno food extends to Bat Yam, the next city in the south.

3 Discover Tel Aviv!

In 2009, Tel Aviv celebrated its 100th birthday. Much has happened since then. The city has increasingly opened up for the growing number of tourists. There are many ways to approach the city: through a city tour, a walk on the beach, following the traces of the Templers and Ottomans or in the shade of great architecture.

3.1 Sight-Seeing Tour

The sight-seeing tour gives a good general overview of the city. With a convertible bus (No. 100), you will see Tel Aviv from north to south in eight languages to choose from. The tour starts in the very north, behind Hangar 4 in the Port of Tel Aviv (exact address: Kaf Gimel Yordey Sira 1). On Friday, the last bus leaves Hangar 4 at 14.00. You can freely hop on and off the bus during the trip; however, the next bus is at least one hour away and might be already full. Here you can see the route:
http://www.dan.co.il/download/files/100Nom.pdf

1.) Leaving from Hangar 4: 09.00, 11.00, 12.00, 13.00, 14.00, 15.00, 16.00

3.2 Guided Walks

The municipality offers free walking tours. The tours are held in English, no registration necessary. During the Jewish holidays, there are no tours.

The White City: Saturdays at 11.00
The tour goes up Rothschild Boulevard and explores the side streets. By strolling up the green boulevard, you will learn about the beginnings of Tel Aviv, the architecture, the city's UNESCO status and the city development of then and now.

2.) Meeting point: 46, Rothschild Boulevard (corner of Shadal St.)

Sarona – Fridays 11.00
From German Templers to Modern Shopping & Chill Out. Enjoy a walk through Sarona, a picturesque historic settlement made of small houses from central Europe. Today, they host well known fashion labels and nice café and restaurants.

3.) Meeting Point: Eliezer Kaplan, 34/ David Elazar St.

4 City Walks

4.1 From Neve Tzedek to Achuzat Beit

At the end of the 19th century, Jaffa started to blossom. The already overpopulated medieval town with its narrow alleys was about to collapse. The demand for flats was very high and the level of hygiene very low. Living in Jaffa would soon turn into a realistic threat to one's health. Under the auspices of Shimon Rokach, Aaron Chelouche (many times transcribed from Hebrew as Shlush), Haim Amzaleg and Zera Barnet, a group of 48 families started a new settlement outside Jaffa. They bought land north-west of Jaffa and founded the first Jewish suburb in 1887 – Neve Tzedek, Oasis of Justice.

The Neve Tzedek neighborhood with its low-rise buildings and the red roofs has maintained (so far) its village character and most of the buildings are still in the original state. This area is full of galleries, museums, restaurants, cafés, bars and little shops. Coming from Jaffa, Neve Tzedek is on the way to Achuzat Beit (original name of Tel Aviv.) If you want to follow the chronological city development, it is best to start at the old railway station, HaTachana, with Jaffa in the back. This is how the founders saw it. On the way to the north, you will discover the little side streets where even today there is no side-walk and time seems to stand still, like in Sharabi Street (extension of Lilienblum Street.) When you have reached the Eden Cinema, you are standing on the border of Neve Tzedek and Achuzat Beit, later re-named Tel Aviv.

1) The old train station – HaTachana

The old train station of Jaffa – HaTachana – is located on the border to Neve Tzedek. The construction of the railway strengthened Jaffa's position as the economic center of

Palestine; in 1892, the first train would run between Jaffa and Jerusalem. In the last years, the station has been thoroughly renovated and stylish boutiques, cafés and restaurants moved into the old buildings. Next door, you find the museum of the Ministry of Defense.

2) Suzanne Dellal Center (6, Yehieli St.)
In the core of Neve Tzedek, you find this dance center in a palace-like setting. Founded in 1989, Dellal organizes today over 750 events throughout the year and is renowned for its modern interpretations. The center is home to different dance companies, like the "Batsheba Dance Company" or the "Inbal Dance Theater."

3) Mosaic
A big mosaic has been dedicated to the founding fathers of Neve Tzedek at the exit of the Dellal Center.

4) The Chelouche House (32, Shlush St.)
Aaron Chelouche (1829-1920) was one of the founding fathers. He had come from Algeria to Palestine and was an influential member of the society. Last but not least, his knowledge of Arabic came in very handy when buying plots of land. His house on 32, Shlush Street was completed in 1886.

5) Shai Agnon's House (2, Rokach St./ 35, Shlush St.)
Nobel Prize winner Shmuel Yosef Agnon (1888-1970) lived in this house from 1909 to 1913. He wrote poetry and short stories in Hebrew and Yiddish in which he portrayed Jewish life in the East-European "Shtetls." In 1966, he had been awarded the Nobel Prize for literature together with the Jewish German writer Nelly Sachs.

6) Amzaleg House (22, Shlush St.)
This beautiful entrance leads to the house of Haim

Amzaleg (1824-1916) who was not only one of the co-founders of Neve Tzedek, but also British vice consul in Jaffa during the reign of the Ottomans (until 1917.) As British citizen, Amzaleg could easily circumvent the law that prohibited the sale of land to Jews. As a British diplomat, he signed the purchase of several hectares of land about 15 km south of Jaffa that he would later sign over to Jewish families. Because of this, 17 Jewish families could lay the corner stone of the city of Rishon Le Zion.

7) The Chelouche Bridge
Aaron Chelouche was the builder of this bridge that once crossed the railway and connected Jaffa and Neve Tzedek.

8) Neve Tzedek Tower (65, Eilat St.)
The construction of the Neve Tzedek Tower made it finally obvious that the "Oasis of Justice" (as Neve Tzedek is translated from Hebrew) will not be able to preserve its village character forever. Several neighborhood groups have been founded to prevent similar projects in the future. Time will tell if that is possible.

9) Walhalla, the Wagner factory
Right next to the Neve Tzedek Tower, there are two little buildings from the Templers, some of the last remaining from the Walhalla settlement that was established here in 1888. When Jaffa started expanding during the economic boom, the Templers also kept an eye out for new plots. Some of the families settled their houses and garages on the border between Neve Tzedek and Jaffa, close to the railway, like Wilhelm and Georg Wagner who produced water pumps.

The Wagner family was one of those Templers who were allowed to re-open their factories after the end of World War II. The Jews were indignant. After the war, the truth about the Nazis had been known to the world. In 1946, Gotthilf Wagner was murdered on Levanda Street in Tel Aviv. The murder case has never been solved, but a Jewish resistance group had been suspected.

10) The Lorenz Café (57, Eilat St.)
The Templer Society of Walhalla had a very lively social life. In No. 57, there used to be the Lorenz Café. Legend has it that this was a popular venue for the meetings of the Rotary Club and that it was the best place to enjoy a draught beer. The Templers were German patriots and were strongly and increasingly infiltrated by the Nazis who would also gather at the Lorenz since the end of the 1920s. In 1925, the Kessem Cinema started showing movies here. With its location on the Jaffa side of town, it was the only competition to the Eden Cinema that had the only concession for Tel Aviv (see "Eden Cinema.")

Since 1970, the building was abandoned. The Schechter Institute for Jewish Culture purchased it in 2011 and completed the renovations in 2012.

11) Former German Consulate (59, Eilat St.)
The German Consulate was located right next to the Lorenz until the beginning of World War II. The proximity to the Templers in Walhalla and the Arabs in Jaffa was of strategic importance for the Nazis in Palestine.

12) The Writer's House (21, Shimon Rokach St.)
Built in 1887, it used to be the seat of the newspaper, HaPoel HaZair. After a successful fight against its demolition, it finally became a museum. It poses many works from Nachum Gutman (1898-1980) who was also famous for his prose, children's books and illustrations. A big mosaic of his is displayed in the hall of the Shalom Tower.

13) The Rokach House (36, Shimon Rokach St.)

Shimon Rokach, one of the founding fathers of Neve Tzedek, built this building in 1887. This house, with its unusual roof, was the first that was finished in the new settlement outside Jaffa. Here, it was his grand-daughter, the sculptor Leah Majaro-Mintz, who prevented it from being torn down. She refurbished the building and opened it later for exhibitions.

14) The Twin Houses (32, Pines St.)

Aaron Chelouche built for his two sons two identical buildings at 30-32, Pines St.; they are called "The Twins."

15) The Eden Cinema (Lilienblum St./ Pines St.)

When the Eden Cinema opened in 1914, the neighbors were not amused. They wrote aggressive letters to the municipality claiming that a place of public entertainment would bring the neighborhood down. The operators, Moshe Abarbanel and Mordechai Weiser, had the exclusive license for the local cinema business for the next 15 years. Nevertheless, another movie theater was opened in 1920 in 57, Eilat Street (10.) Since this was right on the border but officially Jaffa, it did not interfere with the exclusive license for Tel Aviv. The Eden Cinema started with silent films. It was the first movie theater in the country and very successful. Later, an open air movie theater was added and the locals distinguished between the summer- and the winter-Eden. The Eden operated until 1974. The building is protected.

4.2   From Achuzat Beit to Tel Aviv

Under the auspices of Akiva Aryé Weiss, the society "Achuzat Beit" was founded in 1906; a housing company to develop the new settlement the European Zionists were dreaming of. On 11 April 1909, the purchased plots were divided into lots and construction began. In 1910, the name was changed to "Tel Aviv", this was the title Nachum Sokolow had given the Hebrew translation of Herzl's "Altneuland." In the same year, the "Street of the People" – Ha'am Street – was renamed Rothschild Boulevard. Baron Edmond de Rothschild had supported the project financially.

The corner of Herzl Street and Rothschild Boulevard is a good starting point for a discovery walk through the former Achuzat Beit; this is where everything had begun. Herzl Street was the first commercial street while the Boulevard was the place where the founders erected their individual villas in the Eclectic Style. This was the main building style in Achuzat Beit; a bit of the Near East (many houses had orient-style windows) and some decorative elements from the home country (like little Russian towers.) The architecture will change little by little on the way up to the north-east. Take a journey through time from 1909, the year of the groundbreaking, until 1957, when the Friedrich Mann Auditorium was inaugurated.

1) The First Kiosk (Herzl St./ Rothschild Blvd.)
The journey starts at the first kiosk of Tel Aviv. Today, you will see a replica there and the main part of the Boulevard is now home to little bars, cafés and tapas bars that operate from similar kiosks.

2) The Weiss House (2, Ahad Ha'am St./ Herzl St.)
The house of the Achuzat Beit founding father, Aryé Akiva Weiss, was the first in the new settlement. In the following

decades, the house would be altered inside and outside. In the 1920s, another floor was added to the originally single-storied house for residential use by the Weiss family. The ground floor was used commercially. Also the façade was changed over the years. The original design wasn't discovered until the whole building was refurbished in the year 2000.

3) Migdal Shalom/ Gymnasium Herzliya (9, Ahad Ha'am St.)

The Shalom Tower is a controversial office building that can be seen from far away. When it was finished in 1965, it was the highest building in Israel and for a long time in the whole Near East. On 28 July 1909, the cornerstone was laid for the first Hebrew high school in the world– the "Gymnasium Herzliya." Legend has it that architect Joseph Barky had been inspired by the Holy Temple in Jerusalem which led to the Moorish design. In the first years after the founding of the high school in 1906, the students of Yehuda Levi Metman-Cohen (1869-1939) and his wife, Fania, were educated in their private flat in Jaffa. In 1963, the Gymnasium Herzliya moved to a new building in Jabotinsky Street where today an ornamented iron gate commemorates the school's first building from 1909. The first building had been built on a hill and embodied the values of a new Jewish society: no longer as a house of prayer or the center of daily life, but as a house of culture and education.

On the ground floor and the first floor, there is a public exhibition about the first days of Tel Aviv. Even though the documentation is in Hebrew, the old photographs are well worth seeing. The entrance hall displays mosaics of Israeli artists, Nachum Gutman and David Sharir, which tell the city's history.

4) The First Department Store (16, Herzl St.)

Yehuda Magidovitch built here Tel Aviv's first department store in 1925, and the style is very characteristic of the 1920s. On the upper side of the façade, the old name can still be read: "Pensak's Passage."

5) The Shiff House (26, Lilienblum St. / Herzl St.)

Olga and Itzhak Frank built this building in 1909, and in those days it was the "Frank House" as it is noted in the archives. Like most buildings of that time, also the Frank House was not higher than one floor and had a red tiled roof. Later, in the 1920s, the Shiff family bought it, modified it like the Weiss House and also added another storey. Today, the Shiff House is the private bank museum of Bank Diskont which refurbished the building in 2006.

6) Memorial to the Founding Fathers

The memorial at the fountain is dedicated to the first 66 families of the city and was inaugurated in 1951.

They had been the initiators who divided the purchased plots among each other on 11 April 1909, and hence led the cornerstone of Tel Aviv. The east side of Aharon Priver's memorial tells the city's history: the planning of the sand dunes, the Rothschild Boulevard and on the upper end, you will discover Dizengoff Square with its surrounding buildings in the International Style. The other side lists the names of the above mentioned 66 families.

7) Independence Hall (16, Rothschild Blvd.)
On 5 Iyar 5708 (14 May 1948), David Ben-Gurion proclaimed the State of Israel at Rothschild Boulevard. The first mayor of Tel Aviv, Meir Dizengoff, had left this private building of his to the municipality. Today, it is called "Independence Hall" and hosts the museum of the historic events that led to the foundation of the state. The statue in front of the building shows Meir Dizengoff on his horse.

8) The Golomb House (23, Rothschild Blvd.)
This building is from 1913. The owner, Eliyahu Golomb, was the founder of the resistance group, Hagana, and lived here until his death in 1945. At the beginning of the 1960s, the building was taken over by the Ministry of Defense and is today the Hagana Museum.

9) The Lederberg House (29, Rothschild Blvd./ Allenby St.)
Like many other buildings from the 1920s, the Lederberg House was also erected in the Eclectic Style. The façade displays ceramics with biblical themes. Downstairs, the legendary "Benedict's" serves one of the best breakfasts in town.

10) Allenby Street
In the days when Tel Aviv was booming, Allenby Street

became increasingly important as the new commercial center. According to the city development, Allenby Street would also grow longer. The street starts south of Rothschild Boulevard and drops to the sea right behind the Yemenite Quarter. It gave the residents access to the beach without having to traverse the Arabic neighborhood of Manshiye (today Charles Clore Park.)

11) The Great Synagogue (110, Allenby St.)
The centers of the new Jewish society were cultural buildings and not synagogues. Hence, the Great Synagogue opened its doors in 1926 a bit off the city's most important street. It is still Israel's biggest prayer house. The fast and unforeseen growth of the new settlement was disadvantageous for the congregation. Allenby Street would strengthen its position as a commercial center and the residents preferred living in the new residential area that mushroomed in the north. Over there, in the new streets, they would later open little prayer houses. The architect, Aryé Elhanani, was in charge of the building's renovation in 1969 when the new "coat" of pillars was also added. This paid homage to Oscar Niemeyer who had already invented a very similar design in the 1950s for the Ministry of Foreign Affairs in Brasilia.

12) The Palm Tree House (8, Nahalat Binyamin St.)
The "Beit HaDekel" was built in 1922 by architect Yehoshua Zvi Tabechnik. During the 1920s, the local architects were searching for a "Hebrew Style," hence, the Star of David on many buildings façades or balcony ornaments. Here, in No. 8, the menorah is the decorative Jewish element on the upper iron balconies.

13) Bialik Street
This is one of the most interesting streets in the center of Tel Aviv because of its many different building styles.

Bialik and its side streets form together the UNESCO-defined Zone C of the World Heritage area. Here, you find the house of poet Haim Nahman Bialik (No. 22), the Reuben Museum (No. 14), the first city hall (No. 26) and last but not least, the Felicja Blumental Center (No. 26) which houses a comprehensive music library and frequently organizes concerts. On the way to Allenby Street, you will find more buildings from the 1930s in the International Style.

14) King Albert Square
At the junction of Nahmani and Melchett – King Albert Square – not only are streets coming together, but also different architecture styles. The Pagoda House from 1924 combines western and oriental elements, like the 21 Moorish arches. The Shafran House on the corner of Melchett and Nahmani is a typical building for the Eclectic Style. Right on the other side of the street, a construction in the International Style shows up.

15) The Levin House (46, Rothschild Blvd./ Shadal St.)
Zvi Levin, a Lithuanian-born American, made his life-long dream come true when he immigrated to Palestine after retirement. He appointed Yehuda Magidovitch to build his house on Rothschild Boulevard and in 1924, he moved in and lived there until he died in 1935. The house resembled an Italian summer house with neo-classical elements, a popular style at the end of the 19th century. His family decided to go back to the US and sold the Levin House that later became an English school, then Hagana headquarters and finally it was used as the Russian Embassy. The Embassy left the building in 1953 after a bomb blast. Authorities suspected the attack to be a protest against persecution of Jews in Russia. At some point in the 1980s, the house was sold to Alfred Akirov who refurbished the building completely for which he received a construction

permit from the municipality for the office tower behind the building. Until 2006, the Levin House was used by the Sotheby's auction house. Finally, it was sold to the founder of the Heseg Foundation who gives grants to students in Israel.

16) The Engel House (84, Rothschild Blvd.)
The Engel House is one of the prominent representatives of the "Modern Movement." It was the first building in Tel Aviv constructed on pillars, an element that reflects Le Corbusier's influence on local architecture. He was architect Ze'ev Rechter's mentor. When the building plots became scarce, pillar construction was the sophisticated answer to the question of how to maximize use of space without ignoring the mandatory green areas. The roof garden expressed the values of the workers' movement of the 1930s, a space to socialize for all neighbors. The floor plan revolves around a courtyard that opens to the neighboring Mazeh Street.

17) The Rubinsky House (65, Sheinkin St./ Gilboa St.)
With each step, the boulevard is now slowly changing its

architecture and the International Style becomes predominant. Lucian Korngold was mentioned many times as the architect of this building but other sources refer to old documents in the archives that show the names of Marcusfeld & Karnovsky.

18) HaBima (HaBima Square)

HaBima is considered Israel's national theater. It was founded in 1913 in Russia and finally settled in 1931 in Tel Aviv. Its own building was finished in 1945 but the company already moved in before the end of construction. From 2007 to 2010, the building was refurbished and expanded. The original building consisted of a cylinder that now has been integrated into the new cube.

19) The Charles Bronfman Auditorium (1, Huberman)

The architects Ze'ev Rechter as well as Dov Karmi and their respective teams had both sent their own proposals for the auditorium and were surely more than surprised when the jury announced that they want a combination of both and prompted them to work together. The project got funding from Frederic R. Mann (1904-1987) from Philadelphia, USA, an international sponsor of art and music projects. The building was completed in 1957 and is since then the home of the Israeli Philharmonic Orchestra. Unlike most public buildings at that time, the Mann Auditorium has no stairs in front of the entrance and seems to absorb the visitors. In 2013 the name was changed to Charles Bronfman Auditorium. The American billionaire donated $7.7 mio for the renovation of the concert hall.

4.3   Jaffa – The Bride of the Sea

The natural harbor had turned Jaffa already early in history into the economic center of the region and into the focus of many conquerors. Every one of them had left his mark in the city's architecture, like the Ottoman governor (1808-1818) Muhamman Abu-Nabbut who constantly constructed new buildings. Jaffa has always been the melting pot of different cultures and religions and this has not changed. Only about 100 years ago, those little streets were crowded and packed with residents and merchants; today, they are picturesque and home to galleries, restaurants and shops. There is not much left from the original Jaffa and its character. The urban alterations already started during the British Mandate. Streets like Mifrats Shlomo and Luis Pasteur were built in those days when the British tore down houses to widen the streets so they could be accessed with military vehicles. Thanks to a group of artists who would settle in Jaffa later in the 1960s and 1970s, at least a part of the town was preserved. Today, the Old Jaffa invites you to romantic walk in its historic streets.

A tour through Jaffa can be well combined with a visit to the Ilana Goor Museum or a stroll in the flea market, and later you will have the chance to drop by Dr. Shakshuka (3, Beit Eshel St.) to try Israel's national dish: shakshuka.

1) The Clock Tower (Yefet St.)
The clock tower is legendary. It was built in 1906 by Turkish Sultan Abd-el Hamid II who wanted to modernize the country. Fixed hours were considered quite revolutionary in a time when the day was subdivided into dusk and dawn. The clock tower is the most popular meeting point in Jaffa.

2) Kishleh – The Ottoman Prison

The prison of the old Saray (kishleh) was separated from the Saray in 1870 and relocated west of the clock tower. After 1948, it was used as police station until 2006. The relocation of the kishleh happened in a time when Jaffa was growing and the city walls were torn down to help the city expand. Now it is the address of a hotel.

3) The New Saray
At the end of the 19th century, the new Saray was completed, vis-à-vis the kishleh and the Ottoman administration closed the old Saray and moved to the new location. The white ruins are a reconstruction of the original neo-classical building that was bombed during the war of independence on 4 January 1948. Now it is the addresse of the Kishleh Hotel from the Orchid-Group.

4) Sabil Suleiman (Yefet St. at the Clock Tower)
A "sabil" is a public water place either for a ritual washing before the prayers or to refresh after a long journey. Sabil Suleiman was built in 1809 by Suleiman Pasha, the governor of Akko and "boss" of Muhammad Abu-Nabbut. It is located at the southern wall of the Mahmoudiya Mosque.

5) House of the Turkish Governor
The building on the right side of the Saray is the former building of the Turkish governor. During recent years, a concept had been developed to turn the building into a Turkish culture center. The works had already started when in 2010 the diplomatic relations between Israel and Turkey tensed and the project had been adjourned indefinitely due to the Gaza flotilla.

6) The Mahmoudiya Mosque (Roslan St.)

The Mahmoudiya Mosque, built in 1812 by governor Muhammad Abu-Nabbut, is the biggest in the city. Water reservoirs were installed in front of the mosque for the ritual washing. The hidden treasures of the mosque with its courtyards are not accessible for tourists since the mosque is not open for non-Muslim visitors.

7) The Flea Market

A visit to the flea market of Jaffa is a "must." The entrance can be easily found; it is the 2nd street on the left coming up from the clock tower, Oley Zion. In the streets around the flea market, young Israeli designers have their boutiques and ateliers. Not only is the flea market a paradise for bargain hunters, there are more second-hand and antique shops in the neighborhood as well as carpet and silver merchants. You will hear full-throated bargaining left and right; welcome to the Near East! Inside the shops it is a bit quieter, but nowhere else in the cities of Europe and Near East are neighbors so close. The whole area around the flea market is a little vibrant world spiced with nice cafés and restaurants.

8) The Old Saray (8-10, Mifrats Shlomo St.)

In the 19th century, Muhammad Abu-Nabbut expanded the old Saray that was originally built in 1740. It used to be part of a huge administrative structure that once also included a prison and a public bath house. The Ottomans used the building for about 150 years until they moved into a new Saray in 1890 next to the house of the Turkish governor.

9) The Andromeda Rock

This famous rock is located right next to the port of Old Jaffa and can be spotted from the boardwalk. According to the Greek mythology, Andromeda was the daughter of

Egyptian king Cepheus and the Ethiopian queen Cassiopeia. She was tied to the rock to be sacrificed to the sea but was rescued by her future husband, Perseus.

10) St. Peter
The Franciscan church was inaugurated in 1894 after several years of construction. The church is located pictorially on a hill and is the center of attraction for all visitors. The inside is abundantly decorated and the windows are especially well worth seeing. It also houses a painting of St. Peter on the roof of Simon the Tanner whose house is located nearby (19.)

11) Jaffa Visitors' Center
You will find the entrance to the underground visitors' center of Jaffa at Kedumim Square in front of St. Peter's Church. The center is located close to an archeological excavation and shows the long history of Jaffa (http://www.oldjaffa.co.il)

12) Gan HaPisga
The park on the hill (pisga = peak) with its exotic plants and several sculptures is the work of Avarahm Karavan. The "Statue of Faith" by Daniel Kafri and the "Zodiac Bridge" are popular photo motifs. The view from the top is worth the effort.

13) Zodiac Bridge
The balustrade of this short wooden bridge is decorated with the 12 signs of the zodiac. Put your hand on your sign and make a wish!

14) Statue of Faith (Gan HaPisga)
Israeli artist Daniel Kafri created this 4 meter high gate-resembling statue in 1977. It shows the three patriarchs Abraham, Isaac and Jacob in different biblical moments:

Jacob's dream in which the land is promised to his descendents (left), Abraham's sacrifice of Isaac (right) and the fall of Jericho (top).

15) Ramses II's Gate Garden (Gan Sha'ar Ramses)
On the hill of Gan HaPisga you also find the Gate of Ramses II (1,400-1,200 BC) that was discovered during an excavation. This gate shows again the rich history of Jaffa and the political interests of the many conquerors who came here.

16) The Al-Bahr Mosque
The oldest mosque of Jaffa looks back on over 400 years of history; the year of construction is unknown but is estimated to be in the middle of the 16th century. Apparently, the mosque was constructed in different stages and the minaret added at a later time. Legend has it that the wives of the fishermen came here to pray for their safe return. After years without usage, the building was refurbished in 1997.

17) Jaffa Port
This harbor is one of the oldest in the world and soaked  with history. Pilgrims, crusaders, Jewish immigrants, Arab refugees — they all passed the port of Jaffa as well as countless boxes of Jaffa oranges. In 1936, this port would have to face competition for the first time in its history: the Jews built their own harbor in Tel Aviv close to the Yarkon river. Additionally, a modern harbor opened in 1965 in Ashkelon and Jaffa became quiet. Even though the big ships stay away from Jaffa, a new vibe

has been emerging. Galleries and restaurants have reanimated the old port, fishermen are now selling fresh fish here and yachts are offered for sailing trips.

18) Netiv HaMazalot St.

The street of the signs of the zodiac, Netiv HaMazalot, runs parallel to the port. From here you can walk up to the old city with its narrow little streets. Many of them are named after the signs: Tleh (Aries), Shor (Taurus), Teomim (Gemini), Sartan (Cancer), Aryé (Leo), Betula (Virgo), Moznaim (Libra), Akrab (Scorpio), Keshet (Sagittarius), Gdi (Capricorn), Dli (Aquarius), Dagim (Pisces.)

19) Simon the Tanner (Shimon Habourskai St.)

He belongs to the Saints of the Maronite Christian faith and is mentioned in the Acts of the Apostles (9 and 10). According to the Acts, Simon was the landlord of St. Peter. On his rooftop, Peter had a vision that sent him to Caesarea to meet Captain Cornelius, a non-Jew. This is the first biblical hint to an early Christian expansion of the missionary activities outside the Jewish community. This exegesis is debatable as is the location. This house can best be reached once you pass St. Peter's at the end of Kedumim Square. It has been in the possession of the Armenian-Christian family Zarkarian for several generations.

20) The Libyan Synagogue (2, Mazal Dagim St.)

House number 2 is located at the western end of Mazal Dagim Street. When finished in 1749, the building was used as a caravansary and offered accommodation for travelers and their animals. In the Ottoman empire, these places were much more modest than in other parts of the orient; you would even have had to bring your own cutlery and blankets. From 1860 onwards, the building was used by the local population for different purposes. Rabbi Zunana purchased it later to found here a synagogue with a hostel for Jewish pilgrims. The exact year is not known. Years later, the Jews were expelled and were only allowed to pray there when the Arab owner granted them permission. After 1948, the synagogue was given back to the Libyan Jewish congregation. Nowadays, it is only frequented for special events.

21) The Floating Orange (Mazal Aryé St.)

At the eastern end of Mazal Aryé Street, after passing the Richter Art Gallery (No. 24), you will see this exceptional installation: an orange tree floating above the earth. With this work, the artist Ran Morin presents the fusion of nature and technology.

22) St. Georgius (1-5, Louis Pasteur St.)

This Greek Orthodox church from the 19th century is located right on the border with Ajami where Christians from the Near East settled down at the end of the 19th century.

הרובע המרוני
MARONITE QUARTER
حي الماروني

4.4 Ajami

At the end of the 19th century, Jaffa was booming. The economy was strong and there were plans being made for a railway to Jerusalem. It had become crowded in Jaffa, flats were scarce and the expansion of the city became an imperative. Starting in 1870, little by little, the city wall was torn down. The Jews founded Neve Tzedek, the Muslims Manshiye and the Christians went south and settled eventually in Ajami, next to the Muslim neighborhood of al-Jabaliya. On the western side of Yefet Street, the Maronites founded their quarter; on the eastern side, the Copts.

During the War of Independence in 1947/48, most of the Arab citizens of Jaffa left the country and the neighborhood was deserted. With the founding of the State of Israel, Jews got expelled from Arabic states and many found a new home where somebody else had abandoned it. Arabs from other parts of Israel who had not left the country also moved to this area. Over the decades, Ajami got very run-down; the new big beach park, Gan HaMidron, was a dumping place and blocked the view to the sea until recently. The architectonic wealth of the neighborhood was not discovered until the 1980s when investors suddenly had an eye on Ajami and its old villas and palace-like old buildings. New, mainly Jewish neighbors moved in. Since then, the development of the neighborhood has been under fire for its increasing number of luxury condominiums which lead to a further scarcity in affordable flats.

Ajami is located in Jaffa's south. You can discover the Christian neighborhood by entering Ajami in the north and finish at the Givat Aliya Beach from where you can walk back to Jaffa next to the seaside. If you are too tired for a walk, you can also take bus No. 37 that stops above the Peres Peace Center. It will take you back to the Jaffa harbor and continue via Jerusalem Boulevard to the Carmel Market in Tel Aviv. The north-bound bus stop is on Valencia Street (becomes Ibn Sina Street) which is parallel to Kedem Street where the bus stop for the southern route is located.

1) Dolphin Street
Fortified by a hearty breakfast at "Abu Hassan Hummus" (at No. 1) you can now set out on a tour through Ajami. Be there early; once the hummus is sold, the shop closes. Dolphin Street is part of the Maronite Ajami. You will pass an Italian church (at No. 11) that is currently not in use and the Maronite church (at No. 20) which was built by church member Iksander Awad (also known as Alexander Howard) who is buried in the church's court yard.

2) Ytzhak Avineri Street
This street is worth a little detour. In 1855, the Coptic church founded a monastery here. At the intersection of Avineri and Yefet Street (at No. 51), you will see the Catholic St. Anthony's church from 1932 and the neighboring Terra Santa High School. In the immediate proximity, you'll find the Anglican church (Yefet St. 48), also currently not in use.

3) Bathsheba de Rothschild St.
This little side street is hiding at the end the "Scot's House", an old English hospital from the 19th century. In the 1950s, it was closed and later acquired by two Scotsmen who turned it into a hotel.

4) Sha'arei Nikanoor St./ Ziona Tagger St.
Left and right of Yefet Street, you will discover beautiful old houses. At Ziona Tagger Street No. 6, you see a building that belonged to a rich Arab family. The building style is called "Liwan house." These buildings consist of a

big residential area in the middle of the house and various rooms are organized around it. When you cross Yefet Street, make you sure you go by Fakhri Geday's pharmacy at No. 65. This is a true example of the old Jaffa before 1948. The Geday family has been living in Jaffa for many generations and always owned this place.

5) Dudaim St./ Lotus St.
The streets east of Yefet, Dudaim and Tsonobar Street, are well worth a stroll. Magnificent buildings in different architecture styles are waiting for you.

6) 80, Shivte Yisrael St.

This building is very typical of the Jaffa building style of the 19th century: a palace-like generous and elegant structure with inner balconies and decorated pillars. A "Liwan".

7) Toulouse St. 1
Architect Yitzhak Rapaport built this modern building in 1935 for a wealthy Arab family who left the country in 1948. With the architect as mediator, they were able to sell the building to the French Republic before leaving. Since then, it is the residence of the French ambassador to Israel.

8) Givat Aliya Beach
This is the southernmost beach of Tel Aviv. The atmosphere is relaxed and the panorama very different from all the other beaches; to the north there is Jaffa, to the south, Bat Yam. The sea here is rough and the ground

rocky; not the best place for a swim, but definitely for a long beach walk. Several good restaurants with Arabic cuisine can be found in proximity to the beach as well as Jaffa Slope Park that connects this beach with the port.

9) Peres Center for Peace (132, Kedem St.)

This impressive building is a direct neighbor of the Givat Aliya Beach. It seems as if it was contemplating the sea. The massive cube is the design of the Italian architects Massimiliano & Doriana Fuksas and was completed in 2009 after 6 years of construction. The NGO in the Peres Peace Center was founded in 1996 by Israel's President Shimon Peres. The organization supports the dialogue between Jews and Arabs and operates in many fields; in nearly all areas of society, the organization offers help and cooperation: medical services, education, technology, economy, etc. The NGO's philosophy is that peace only happens between people and not organizations.

10) Gan HaMidron

This park of approximately 50 hectares is the second biggest of Israel after Yarkon Park and is one of the most comprehensive recycling projects. Nothing seems to remind the visitor of the city's dumping ground that was here until 2010. Today, you see a green oasis next to the sea, ideal for jogging and biking and equipped with nice playgrounds. The park connects Jaffa with the Givat Aliya beach, the ultimate place for a beach walk.

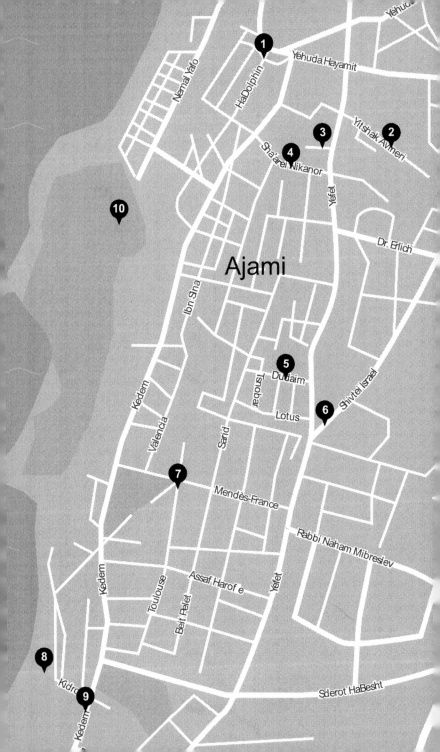

4.5 Historic Beach Walk

Walking along Tel Aviv's beaches is also a journey through the city's young history. It is convenient to walk the tayelet (Hebrew for "beach front") from south to north. This way, you follow the 100 years of city history chronologically and avoid sunburn.

1) HaTachana
The old train station of Jaffa, HaTachana, is the perfect start for a walk northward. Only a few years ago, this compound had been refurbished and built up again. It is located in the former district of Manshiye. Jaffa's position as the economic center of Palestine benefited significantly from the railway to Jerusalem. At the end of the 19th century, it started to expand. From 1870 on, the city walls were torn down to support the expansion. North of Jaffa, the new district of Manshiye was founded.

2) The Etzel House
The last survivors of Manshiye are the Etzel Museum across from the old train station, the "Red House" on the compound and last but not least, the Hassan Bek Mosque. After the ruins of Manshiye had been torn down in the 1960s, the plan was to turn this area into Tel Aviv's business district. But things changed, and today the Israeli economy is represented next to the Ayalon highway on the border to Ramat Gan in the east. Between 1947 and 1948, Jews and Arabs competed for dominance in Palestine. At the end of April 1948, the resistance group Irgun (Etzel) conquered Manshiye. The residents of Jaffa could see the explosions from far away. As a sign of victory, the Israeli flag was hoisted on top of the Hassan Bek Mosque. Manshiye was conquered.

3) The Charles Clore Park/ Manshiye
With the new plans for the future city development, the

ruins of Manshiye were finally torn down and this district would totally be erased in 1963. In 1974, the Charles Clore Park was inaugurated and modernized in 2007. The name honors the British financier and philanthropist Charles Clore (1904-1979) whose investment group also included the English department store Selfridges. His "Clore Foundation" supports Jewish projects in Great Britain and abroad as well as museums and art collections.

4) The Hassan Bek Mosque

Hasan Bek became the new Ottoman mayor of Jaffa in the summer of 1914. The mosque of Manshiye that was built in 1916 is named after him. Later in history when the aggressions between Jews and Arabs were on the rise, there were repeated sniper attacks on Jews from the minaret of the mosque. The mosque had not been used for a long time and was finally given back to the Muslim community in 1980s. Today's minaret is double the height of the original which broke down in 1983.

5.) Delphinarium

For the Israeli society, the Dolphinarium remains a trauma. A tragedy happened here on 1 June 2003, when a suicide bomber attacked inside the discotheque. 21 people, mostly teenagers, died in the attack and 132 were injured. In front the Dolphinarium, a memorial stone in Hebrew, Russian and English remembers the victims. On the sign behind the stone, two young people are holding hand and the text says "We will not stop dancing.".

Even more than a decade later, there is still a website memorizing the victims (http://www.dolphi.org) as well as annual memorial services are held at the site. For years, the city hall wanted to tear down the dolphinarium. Now, the days of the building finally seem to be counted. In December 2014, a hotel project was approved to be built here within the next years.

6) Border Tel Aviv–Jaffa
During the British Mandate, Daniel Street was the border between Jaffa and Tel Aviv. On 1 May 1921, two Jewish groups violently clashed during Labor Day demonstrations. Both groups were knocking each other around when suddenly an Arab group gathered to beat up the Jews; the violence escalated and led to shootings. The civil population organized themselves and sealed off Tel Aviv. In the following days, they picked up the remaining Jews in Jaffa and cast out Arabs from Jewish neighborhoods. Daniel Street would repeatedly be the venue of conflicts between Jews and Arabs also later in history.

7) 1 Allenby Street/ Knesset Square/ Opera Tower
1 Allenby is an historic address. It used to be the seat of the Knesset (until 1 December 1949) and later of the Israeli National Opera (1958-1982.) The construction work for this building started in 1990 and its name is reminiscent of the golden times of the Israeli Opera and the square in front, reminiscent of the first year after the foundation of the State of Israel: the Opera Tower at Knesset Square. On 19 of 23 floors, there are luxury flats with a private pool on the rooftop. In the lower part of the building, there is a shopping mall with several movie theaters.

8) London Square
Right behind the Orchid Hotel, you will find a little garden with sculptures like ships. This is the memorial for the Aliya Bet (in Israel, "ha-apala"), the "illegal" immigration of Jewish refugees. Historic photos and documentation explain the events. On the eve of the Reichskristallnacht – night of the broken glass – the government of the British Mandate published the 1939 White Paper that also

contained the quota of Jewish refugees that were allowed to enter Palestine in the coming years. A subdivision of the HAGANA, Mossad le Aliya Bet, organized the clandestine immigration of Jewish refugees from Europe between 1938 and May, 1948. More than half of them were stopped by the British Navy. If they were lucky, they were sent mainly to refugee camps in Cyprus, but other ships were sent back to Europe, a death sentence for the passengers.

9.) DAN Hotel

The colorful façade is the curtain behind which hides a true German-Jewish success story: the former "Pension Käthe",

a hostel owned by Käthe Danielewicz. Architect Lotte Cohen, originally from Berlin, had built Käthe's hostel here, a renowned accommodation in Tel Aviv with 21 rooms that was later sold to the

Federmann brothers in 1947. They kept the name and built up a well-known hotel chain, Dan Hotels, with currently 14 hotel properties. Still today you can find the "KD" on the façade.

10.) Abie Nathan (south of the Renaissance Hotel)

 Follow the beach walk downstairs, in the direction of the Renaissance Hotel. Shortly before you arrive at the hotel, you will find a little memorial plaque on the wall and a built-in loudspeaker. Abie Nathan (1927-2008) was an Israeli peace activist and founder of the radio station "Voice of Peace." On 28 February 1966, Nathan flew from Israel to Egypt with his own little plane – Shalom One – to present to President Nasser his ideas about peace talks between Israel and Egypt. He got arrested on his arrival and was sent back to Israel where he was arrested again, but later not sentenced. He kept on trying during the years of 1967 and 1968, and each time the Egyptians would send him back to Israel where he ultimately served a short prison sentence. In 1973, he bought a ship from which he operated the pirate station "Kol Shalom" (Voice of Peace.) Outside Israeli waters, he broadcasted pop music and got actively engaged for peace in the Near East. In 1978, he would repeatedly meet up with the PLO for which he also served a prison sentence in Israel. The radio station was very popular but had to close down on 1 October 1993 due to financial difficulties. Abie Nathan received the International Human Rights Award of Nuremberg in 1997. An online radio station has picked up Nathan's idea and created an acoustic memorial for him: http://www.thevoiceofpeace.co.il .

11) Wall Paintings Gordon Pool

Close to Gordon Street, the walls at the beach front are decorated with nice paintings of bathers. This is where the first swimming pool of Tel Aviv had been, the Gordon Pool. The new pool is located a bit further north.

12.) Arlozorov Memorial

Across from the entrance of the Carlton Hotel, you will see a green tarnished sculpture in memory of Chaim Arlozorov (1899-1933.) The Arlozorovs were Ukrainian Jews who had immigrated to Germany in 1905. Chaim and his

parents had lived in Eisenacher Straße in Berlin-Kreuzberg. He had been fascinated by Zionism but until his permanent move to Palestine in 1924, he had been very close to the woman who would later be known as Magda Goebbels

(maiden name: Behrend.) Once in Palestine, he climbed the social ladder and became the head of the Mapai party and the right hand of Chaim Weitzman. After a dinner with his wife in the Dan Hotel, Arlozorov was shot at the beach of Tel Aviv in June 1933. This murder had never been solved. In recent years, researchers uttered suspicions that the clues could lead to Germany and that this contract murder might have been the revenge of an unfulfilled love (see: "Qui a tué Arlozoroff" by Tobie Nathan, published so far only in French, ISBN-13: 978-2246751311)

13.) Independence Park / Gan HaAtzmaut

From the hill next to the Hilton Hotel, this little park overlooks the sea. It is a nice spot for a romantic sunset. In 1952, the park was offered to the municipality by a private person. Finally in 2009, the area was refurbished for the 100-year celebration of Tel Aviv. Today, the park is home to several sculptures and a little playground.

14) Tel Aviv Port

A new harbor was another significant step towards independence and construction started on 17 May 1936. Between Haifa and Jaffa, there was no other port until then. The coast was very shallow and big ships came as close as they could, but passengers and goods had to be brought ashore by rowboats. The local economy boomed and at the same time more and more immigrants came from Europe; unloading a ship took longer each time and sometimes the ships would have to wait for days until they got unloaded. By 1949, the municipality decided to expand the port activities and deepened the harbor to allow the ship to land and stop the unloading at sea. Today the port is an attractive place with good restaurants, coffee shops and a buzzing nightlife.

15) The Yarkon Estuary

The Yarkon River presented a natural barrier in the fight between the British and the Ottomans. In the night of 20/21 December 1917, the British troops crossed the river and defeated the enemy by surprise. Because of the flood, the Turks had felt secure on the other side. Close to the lighthouse ruins, a stone column is reminiscent of this event.

16) The Lighthouse

On 13 December 1934, two ships collided in front of the Jaffa port. Soon after this accident, this lighthouse was constructed, starting in January 1935, to improve the situation at the shallow coast.

17) The Reading PowerStation

The red lights of the Reading power plant are very visible at night. For a long time, this was the northern end of Tel Aviv until the expansion beyond the Yarkon River. The newly constructed beachfront of Reading passes the airport of Sadeh Dov.

18.) Airport Sadeh Dov

With the intensifying conflict between Arabs and Jews, it became increasingly dangerous for Jews to travel outside the city. The then-mayor of Tel Aviv, Israel Rokach, asked the Mandate government for permission to build Tel Aviv's own airport. Sadeh Dov was finished in 1938 and offered regular flights to Haifa. The airport still serves national flights and is also used by the military, but those days are counted. The military announced the closing of the airport for end of 2015, two years earlier than planned, to give way for the construction of new flats. We will see.

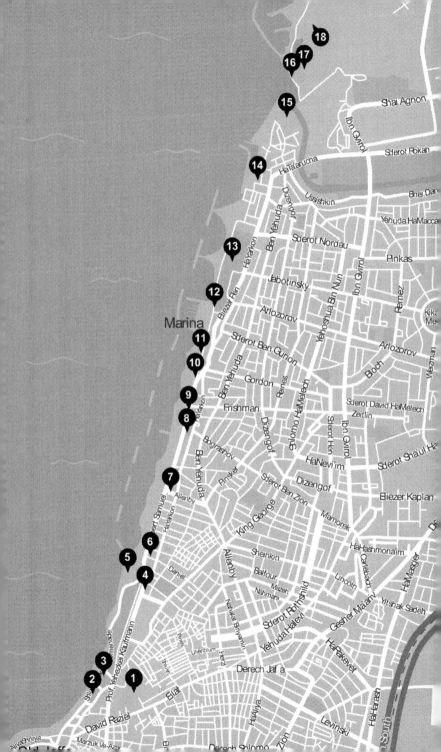

4.6   UNESCO World Heritage

In 2003, UNESCO awarded Tel Aviv the World Heritage status and recognized the world's biggest coherent ensemble of buildings from the 1930s that were constructed in the International Style. All over Tel Aviv, square-edged houses with round balconies can be found. UNESCO subdivided the city center into zones: A (between Ben-Gurion Boulevard and Bograshov St.), B (around Bialik St.) and C (upper Rothschild Boulevard and Nahmani St., up to the Charles Bronfman Auditorium.) Together, they form "The White City" with about 4,000 International Style buildings, many still in need of refurbishment today. The municipality made concessions for the refurbishments and allowed the investors to add one or two floors. The original buildings never exceeded three or four floors. The UNESCO-defined zones are home to 2,087 buildings of which 699 are listed.

The following buildings are representative of this era. Most of the buildings are very centrally located, others a bit off the beaten path but worth the walk. Even those buildings that are in a deplorable state still give an idea of the glamour and the spirit of the old times. Stroll through the streets of the White City and breathe the air of nostalgia.

1) 84, Rothschild Boulevard, Engel House (1934), architect: Ze'ev Rechter

The Engel House is a very prominent representative of the "Modern Movement"; it was the first building on pillars in Tel Aviv, a clear style element from Le Corbusier with whom the architect Ze'ev Rechter had worked during his studies in Paris. When the plots became scarce, the pillar construction was the best compromise to construct as much a possible without neglecting the mandatory green area. The roof garden was a symbol of the workers' movement of the 1930s, a space for encounters with the neighbors.

The U-shaped floor plan includes a courtyard to the neighboring Mazeh Street.

2) 33-35, Frishman St., workers' residence (1935), architect: Arieh Sharon

Arieh Sharon is considered the father of Israeli architecture. He is also the architect of many kibbutzim and made history as David Ben-Gurion's chief planner to build up Israel. This residence is a very interesting and rare combination of residential building and kibbutz. The workers lived in spartan flats and the mutual activities took place in the basement. As in a kibbutz, there was a mensa and around the courtyard – this building is also u-shaped – the laundry, the kindergarten and the shop for daily supply could be found. Sharon had been a student of the Bauhaus school in Dessau. From his master, the architect Hans Meier, he had adopted the belief that architecture is supposed to improve society.

3) 23, Pinsker St., Mintz & Elenberg House (1935), architect: Philip (Pinchas) Hütt

This house is also known as the "anchor house" in reference to the overall impression of the façade. The staircase is illuminated by the glass elements, a signature of the International Style. The buildings had been originally planned for single women, with 35 little flats.

4) 65, Hovevei Zion St., Mirenberg House (1935), architects: Philip (Pinchas) Hütt

The fusion of two building blocks, as is shown in this construction, is another very typical element of the International Style. Two heavy and independent construction blocks are joined by rounded corners and a shared staircase. The often-found asymmetry is underlined by overhanging wings and integrated balconies.

5) 79, Mazeh St., Recanati House (1935), architects: Shlomo Liaskovski & Yakov Orenstein

The spectacular façade design acts on the idea of "functional asymmetry": a dynamic façade for a dynamic street and a neutral, calm composition for the quiet side street. The figurative element of the repetition of the balconies plays with the natural antithesis of light and shadow. The Bar Orian architecture firm completely refurbished the building in 2000.

6) 22, HaRakevet St., Citrus House (1935), architect: Carl Rubin

The Beit Hadar as it is known in Hebrew shows the influence Mendelsohn had on his student, Carl Rubin. It was the first building with a steel skeleton in Tel Aviv. Three independent, massive constructions seem monstrous and heavy and still, yet they seem to be floating on top of the floor. This illusion is created by the use of the windows on the entire façade on the first floor. Glass was often used to visually mark a separation, here: the shops and the offices.

7) 27, Menachem Begin Road, Gavrilovich House (1936), architects: Y. Kashdan & E. Shimshoni

This building is an example of how freely the architects of the International Style were actually "modeling" their houses. This unusual concept plays with light and shadow, squares and circles as well as with concave and convex. The impression of symmetry and asymmetry is not clear anymore. It seems as if one part of the building was cut out and put back as balconies.

8) Idelson St. 29, Max-Liebling-House (1936), architect: Dov Karmi

When Dov Karmi came back from his studies in Belgium, he would surprise the local market with a new style element: immersed balconies. In summer, they protect from too much sun and heat but in winter, they let light and warmth in. The pillar construction introduced by Ze'ev Rechter allowed building without supporting walls and allowed a free planning of the floor and the façade.

9) Zina Dizengoff Square (1936), architect: Gina Averbuch

The conceptual design of Kikar Zina Dizengoff – as the square is correctly called in Hebrew – is the result of a competition like all the public places and buildings. The winner, Gina Averbuch, offered the best solution for a mutual design for both the square and surrounding buildings. The uniform façade design glamorized the square and gave it a harmonious overall picture. In the original blue print, it was foreseen to elevate the center of the square and to create parking space. This feature was not realized and the square became a roundabout. Decades later, the traffic on Dizengoff Street became a challenge and in 1978, the decision was taken to remodel the square with an underpass. This step diminished a lot the main character of the square. Currently, the municipality is studying the possibility to return to the original blue print. Zina Dizengoff was the mayor's late wife.

10) 14, Ben Ami St./ 8, Beilinson St., Kupat Cholim building (1938), architect: Josef Neufeld

The building that is nowadays home to the Kabbala Center was the first seat of the Kupat Cholim, the public health insurance. The original division was based on a functional subdivision of the building with the laboratories and storage in the basement and the offices on the upper floors. The sunken balconies offer shade and perfect ventilation and in winter; when the sun altitude is much lower, light and warmth still enter the rooms.

11) 1, Zamenhoff St., Esther Cinema (1939), architects: Yehuda & Rafael Magidovitch

The façade design follows exactly the concept suggested by Gina Averbuch for the Dizengoff square. The cinema was built for 1,000 spectators and inaugurated in 1939 with Walt Disney's film, "Snow White and the Seven Dwarfs." It became a reference for cultural life in Tel Aviv. From 1998 to 2000, the building was thoroughly refurbished and later a boutique hotel moved in. The hotel is reminiscent of the cinematic past of this place: the whole place is decorated with exhibits from the former cinema, not only the lobby, but also the rooms.

4.6.1 New building, old appearance

Tel Aviv's rediscovered identity with the International Style architecture had led to a boom of façade designs in that old style. A growing number of new buildings have been constructed in a design that directly refers to the 1930s. Many times, it is difficult to estimate the period in which a building was constructed. A good example of these new buildings in old appearance is the corner of Tchernichovsky and Dizengoff Street:

12) 69-73, Dizengoff St./ 59, Tchernichovsky St.

In 2001, the architects Ronit and Elisha Rubin built this

apartment building with its 23 flats on 4 floors. Like the Recanati House (79, Mazeh Street), this building has two different façade designs with different characters: a dynamic, "loud" one on the side facing Dizengoff Street and a much sober design toward the calm side street Tchenichovsky.

4.7   Botanical Garden

The Botanical Garden of the University of Tel Aviv allows visitors to get close to the still unanswered questions of science. Divided into 16 different areas - spread over 34,000 m² - the University shows amazing facets of their research, such as the root research in the Sarah Racine Root Laboratory. About half of the area belongs to Noah Naftulski garden for Israeli plants. The small country of Israel has several climatic regions like the Mediterranean, the desert or the mountain area and thus a variety of plant species. By walking through the cactus forest, the visitor learns how plants behave in arid and salt-rich regions on the different continents. Especially popular is the visit to the tropical house with its orchids, creepers and the humid tropical climate. The Botanical Garden does not not only serve as research field but also helps to preserve endangered plants.

The visit to the garden is free. If you are interested in a guided tour, please contact
Campus *Teva* (in English *nature*): Tel. 03-640.5148, http://www.campusteva.tau.ac.il, teva@tauex.tau.ac.il

How To Get There
The Botanical Garden can be easily reached by **bus 25** which runs every 15 minutes. It stops in front of the entrance, at gate 2 (bus stop "Bait Hatefuzot / Klausner St."). The Diaspora Museum (Bait Hatefuzot) is also located at this stop.

The following is a selection of stops in the city center, where you can get on the bus (direction north!):

1.) Great Synagogue/ Allenby St. 110
2.) Carmel Markt/ Allenby St.
3.) King George/ HaHashmonaim (close to Gan Meir Park)
4.) King George/ Masrik Square
5.) Ibn Gvirol/ Rabin Square
6.) Ibn Gvirol/ Pinkas

Entrance:
7.) Klausner Street, vis-à-vis gate 2.

Opening hours: Su.-Th. 08.00-16.00, the tropical house closes at 14.30.

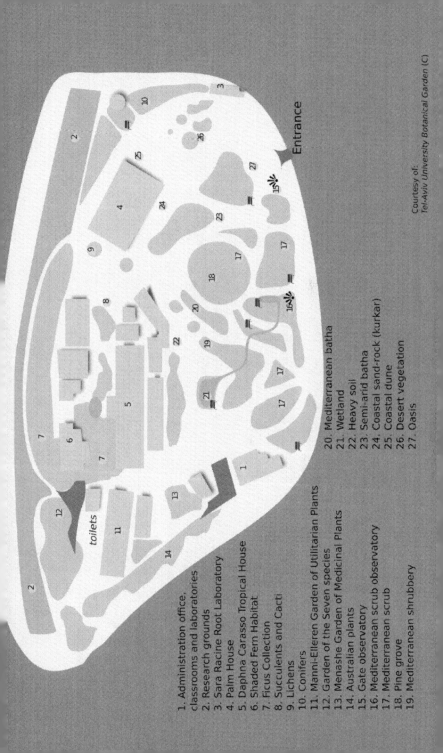

Entrance

1. Administration office,
   classrooms and laboratories
2. Research grounds
3. Sara Racine Root Laboratory
4. Palm House
5. Daphna Carasso Tropical House
6. Shaded Fern Habitat
7. Ficus Collection
8. Succulents and Cacti
9. Lichens
10. Conifers
11. Manni-Elleren Garden of Utilitarian Plants
12. Garden of the Seven species
13. Menashe Garden of Medicinal Plants
14. Australian plants
15. Gate observatory
16. Mediterranean scrub observatory
17. Mediterranean scrub
18. Pine grove
19. Mediterranean shrubbery
20. Mediterranean batha
21. Wetland
22. Heavy soil
23. Semi-arid batha
24. Coastal sand-rock (kurkar)
25. Coastal dune
26. Desert vegetation
27. Oasis

5 Maps for mobile devices

The maps published in this book are the artwork of the author. Additionally, the walks were added to Google Maps, so you can import them to your mobile device. The publication of links to GoogleMaps is in line with their terms of use.

Sightseeing Bus & Guided Walks:
https://goo.gl/DATPx3

From Neve Tzedek to Achuzat Bayit:
https://goo.gl/DDkIyp

From Achuzat Bayit to Tel Aviv:
https://goo.gl/wxcCz2

Jaffa – the Bride of the Sea:
https://goo.gl/bBMAFf

Ajami:
https://goo.gl/CrdPzG

Historical Beach Walk:
https://goo.gl/4PxVWs

UNESCO
https://goo.gl/g8oY9D

Botanical Garden
https://goo.gl/MteJSt

6 Index